Early Bird Reflections

& how not to be
the weakest link

Artwork and text
by Tony Spearing

Thanks

In addition to their similarity of spelling, opinions and onions do have something in common. Eat them (or cousin garlic) raw and it's not only one's breath which could be offputting, but one's views as well.

That's why, as a safeguard, I always write mine down, sucking a peppermint at the same time.

But don't *be* put off. All my opini-onions have been well guinea-pigged by sensitive souls who are, so far, still friendly, having not yet bitten the hand that fed them.

So, grateful thanks to those anonymous friends on the Reading Committee (no upset tums I hope) who have apparently felt no urge to 'roast' me or my onions. Also to David Marshall, one of the gentlest, kindest of editors I've ever had the honour to work with. And almost last but certainly not least, Ron Surridge.

For without Ron's initiative and encouragement, this little collection of 'recipes' would never have seen the light of any kitchen or anywhere else for that matter.

P.S. Not to forget (she's sure I do) my long-suffering, darling wife, who has put up with years of antisocial behaviour in order that Tone's tiny tome could be produced.

Early Bird Reflections

& how not to be the weakest link

by Tony Spearing

Foreword

Relax and welcome to a quiet read written with great warmth by Tony Spearing, a devout Christian and a man of many parts.

A talented artist by profession – it was through this that our own paths crossed when he joined the best-selling women's magazine, *Woman's Weekly*, later to become Art Editor – his interests are numerous and running alongside his love of art and music is his enthusiasm for writing. This he does for his own pleasure, but now most happily he is sharing with us a series of inspirational pieces that are full of wit and wisdom.

Written in comfortable everyday language they are threaded through with Tony's own attractive sketches adorning these pages. Here are subjects to savour and maybe ring a bell in your own lives.

Mary Dilnot Ruffle OBE
Retired Editor Woman's Weekly

First published in 2004
Copyright © 2004
All rights reserved. No part of this publication
may be reproduced in any form without
prior permission from the publisher.
British Library Cataloguing in Publication Data.
A catalogue record for this book is available
from the British Library.
ISBN   1 903921 22 8

Bible versions used:
JBP = J. B. Phillips
GNB = Good News Bible
KJV = King James Version
NIV = New International Version

Published by Autumn House, Grantham, England
Printed in Thailand

Contents

Introduction

One of my early attempts at an interview was with an illustrator who was a great favourite with the readers of the women's magazine I worked for. Unusually, I was actually included in a photograph used of the artist, printed to accompany the article.

I was waiting at my doctor's surgery when a lady sitting opposite picked up our magazine and flicked it open to my article. Nonchalantly trying to feign a headache by shielding my eyes I peered through my fingers with nervous embarrassment.

Would she recognise me?

Illusions of vainglory vanished in a flash. Giving it only a cursory glance she quickly turned on to the back page and became avidly engrossed in reading letters to our agony aunt. I'd agonised too, as I do over much that I've written; and this effort was no exception. It was gratifying that at least I'd been paid (for every single word in fact), but one longs for something more out of life than financial gain.

Isn't there an element of vainglory in most of what we do?

As a Christian, I try to suppress the longing I have to savour the delights of a gracious 'well done', even the shadow of a reward. Nevertheless, I still long to please God and my fellow man, and we all, from childhood onward, surely find it almost impossible to produce or create anything without encouragement.

I grew up with the King James Bible and cherish Revelation 4:11: 'For thou hast created all things, and for thy pleasure they are and were created.'

When I retired and there was no need to get up early in the morning I would often, very irritatingly, find myself wide awake just before dawn. It's a magical hour. Birds are awake too and their songs, so lovely and beautiful, are to my mind an evocation to the glory and honour of God, and seem to demonstrate a spontaneous, instinctive desire to please their own, and our Creator.

I wanted to join in those choruses. I wanted to please God.

That was reward in itself. So I'd get up quietly, nuzzle a cup of tea, open my Bible and write down whatever thoughts would come, delving back into the past, all that I've ever heard or read about God. Hoping to relate, through humorous anecdotes, something worth knowing about the Saviour God I've got to know throughout my life.

Have I succeeded? I don't know yet, though I am confident that the cheeky chirruping of a scruffy old sparrow like me (increasingly rare I might add) *can* raise a smile, or a grimace at least, from anyone who has the tenacity to plough through my verbiage.

But will I succeed in adding anything new or edifying to your inner, spiritual life?

It's for you to decide.

I can only hope and pray.

And of course I will.

A foot on the exaggerator!

My wife is Austrian – bless her – and our family and I are forever grateful that it's not only our diet that's been enriched, but our vocabulary as well.

Posting a letter for instance: *going to the 'pillow box'*. Driving a car: *putting a foot on the 'exaggerator'* with both hands on the *'stirring wheel'*. My braces were a bit lopsided once and I was advised to adjust my *'brassiere'*!

Austrians don't make VWs – they make WVs and our kids grew up thinking a windscreen wiper was a kind of snake.

When we got married she was an alien. *Dad's Army* was a recent memory. A friend queried her accent – *'German?'*

'No – *Austrian!'*

'Oh, that's all right then.'

Mr Hitler had kidded most people about his true nationality.

Germans were the 'nasties' then; but are today's 'nasties' confined to one country? They're everywhere. Racialism and nationalism don't just mean hating your neighbour, but destroying his home or killing him.

Let's face it. Aren't we, as Christians, aliens too? This world is enemy country, but let's be sure we know who the enemy is! And often our greatest enemy is ourselves!

My mum-in-law was lovely, not one of your proverbials. She left us many pearls of wisdom. One was likening a piano keyboard, with its black and white keys, to God's children – on whom he wants to play harmonious music. For we are all one in Christ Jesus (Galatians 3:28).

Pianos are great for playing chords. You can make up a chord from only the white notes, or only the black notes, but it's a combination of both that sounds best. However, the vital thing is that even if you think you are following the composer's instructions, when some of the notes are out of tune – it sounds dreadful!

Open up a piano and you'll see strings attached to pegs. Pegs that must be embedded in a stable, solid foundation, otherwise they'll always be going out of tune.

J. S. Bach wrote two sets of music known as *The Well-Tempered Clavichord*. Not really to do with bad temper or irritability, but tuning. Bach was proving that the then new system based on *Equal Temperament* (or tuning) worked. And how!

It's heavenly music!

You and I are notes on God's piano. Do we have an individual temperament? Or an equal temperament? Are the sounds coming out of your life, out of your church, harmonious? Or is it time we all had another visit from the Heavenly Piano Tuner?

'Fulfil ye my joy, that ye be likeminded, having the same love, being of one accord, of one mind.'

(Philippians 2:2, KJV.)

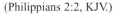

Pear-shaped

Question: What have birth and death got in common?
Answer: Nothing.

My grandson asked me why it is that I'm always starting off my same old stories (which he's heard a hundred times before) with: 'When I was a boy. . . .'

I was stumped for a minute. On the point of offering up that perennial excuse: most grandads are addleheaded (which he knows), I said instead, 'Because as you get older and older your own childhood seems nearer.'

Now there are obvious parallels between old age and childhood. Both are vulnerable. Both have degrees of dependency.

My daughter applied for a care assistant post in an old people's home. Asked about experience, she said: 'Only with children, as a nursery nurse.'

'You'll find it very much the same here,' she was told.
'Only this lot don't run around so much.'

Is it possible to account for this interesting phenomenon?
I doubt it, though I'll try. On condition that it's accepted that
I fuddle. Any hypothesis that I expound must be treated with
the lack of seriousness it deserves.

I think pears are a lovely shape (and I'm not hoping to
endear myself to many of the so-shaped fairer sex). But I do
like those (the fruit I mean) that are elongated at the top. So
imagine this beautiful, symmetrical pear, drawn in outline,
narrow at the top, broad at the base.

This is our model; our graph if you like, showing how man,
despite all his endeavours to make life a progression, will
inevitably (as he uses up most of his allotted life span) find
himself in a state of regression.

Regression?

Yes! It's the word psychologists use to describe the adoption, by an adult, of behaviour more appropriate to a child.

Now is the adoption voluntary or involuntary? I go for the
latter.

Okay. We enter life at the top of our pear shape naked.
We bring nothing into this world and register our annoyance
with a yell of protest.

During our teen age we're still sliding down the narrow bit
and as our pear curves round into the ample, generous bottom,
we're on the way into that region of life known as 'middle
age'. Hence the tendency to 'spread'.

One day we find that everything appears to have moved
uphill. Formerly easy tasks need twice the effort. As Bertie
Wooster aptly puts it, 'Not much bounce to the ounce.' Or, to
be pc, 'Less wham per gram.'

Of course, by now, we're on the other elongated bit again,
but this time inching upwards. And, although (graphically
speaking) in close proximity to childhood again, granted the
grand appellation of 'senior citizens'.

But can't you see that those carefree days of sunny child-hood (with its squeals of joyful delight) are still echoing for us? Just over the gentle rainbow hill of our pear horizon? This is the moment when my nonsensical riddle should make sense.

What have birth and death got in common? Nothing! The Nothing Door.

For we make our exit through the very same door where we came in. It's the door that allows nothing in, and nothing out. *'We leave this world just as we entered it – with nothing. In spite of all our work here there is nothing we can take with us. It isn't right! We go just as we came.'* (Ecclesiastes 5:15, 16, GNB.)

Will there be a figure dressed in black, looking a little like Anne Robinson, saying, 'And *you* Tony Spearing, leave with absolutely nothing'?

Oh dear! Is there no hope of another way out? No! Not unless we can find the door to the Kingdom of Heaven. But man can't possibly find it – can he?

'Unless', as Jesus tells Nicodemus, *'he is born again.'* (John 3:3.)

The new spiritual birth reveals a new door.

'I am the door,' says our Saviour, *'by me if any man enter in, he shall be saved, and shall go in and out.'* (John 10:9, KJV.)

Solomon tells us something we've never wanted to know. That our bodies will return to the dust of the earth and the breath of life will go back to God who gave it to us. The Philosopher further sums up life as dismally useless.

Asa Nonymous, another prolific enlightener, tells us that 'Career is a horse arriving riderless at the gate of Eternity.' I'm so glad I never took up riding.

So what's the point? What can we gain from life?

It's a futility only put into perspective when we know Jesus Christ. Accept his invitation to heaven in John 3:16. Life has no purpose otherwise.

No one feels comfortable talking about death. Inevitable for all, of course. Unless Christ returns for the second time *before* we open our last, earthly exit door. For the believer who trusts his Saviour, death is only a 'holy hibernation' (1 Thessalonians 4:13, 14). Without faith, mankind's egress remains a gateway to nihility. Prosaically, one should term it a bedroom door. That's far too ordinary. God's grace transforms death into a no-shame-infinity door.

True, once we enter, we'll go to sleep (1 Corinthians 15:50-54). Wake up to the eternal reality of being not what we were (just creatures of God's creation), but heirs to his kingdom! Faith in God's only begotten Son finally substantiates its purpose. Our Rescuer embraces us as 'family'. Sons and daughters of our heavenly Father.

'Fear not, for I have redeemed you; I have summoned you by name; you are mine.'

(Isaiah 43:1, NIV.)

Winners and losers

Well, surely it's an easy enough mistake. Both bottles are about the same shape and size in clear glass, so that you see the orange-coloured liquid inside. How was I to know it wasn't what I thought it was?

There was the missus, in a hospital bed. Miles from home. All she did, poor thing, was to ask me trustingly to pour her a drink.

Instinctively the automatic pilot in me took over. Orange squash – must be shaken – says so on the label (at least it usually does).

So I did!

No one told me it was Lucozade.

Extraordinary how much energy can be generated by a few feeble shakes.

Yellow, sticky, frothy, sweet fluid squirted everywhere. Over me, my wife, the bedclothes, the floor, the locker. Even a thoughtful neighbour's flowers and two get-well cards benefited.

Hospital wards have a noise level characteristically increased at visiting time. It's a kind of conversational drone. A rumble-mumble-rhubarb-crumble drone that uncannily ceased after my little calamity. Like loss of sound on the telly. A pregnant silence.

I was busy mopping up with tissues when I became aware of a presence.

Admittedly, I was hoping for the manifestation of one of those National Health Service angels. The mercifully sweet, ray-of-sunshine type. Instead, I got what I deserved.

A grim angel of retribution.

I didn't dare look up at her; didn't need to. My mind's eye saw it all. Arms akimbo. I could feel her basiliskical stare petrifying me at five paces.

Three words entered the ether. Quietly enunciated, but so judgemental!

'Who brought *him*?'

In other words, whoever you are, wherever you are, *please, please* come forward and take him away!

I'd never thought that three simple words could be so devastating.

I wanted to step out there, centre stage, onto the highly polished ward floor, perform a few fantastic flourishes of fabulous footwork in best River Dance tradition, and, with a meek self-effacing bow, acknowledge the standing ovation (of the visitors at least). Plonker that I am, however, I'd come in the wrong footwear – hadn't I?

I wanted, rightly or (more than likely) wrongly, to assert myself. Proclaim to the whole ward that no one brought me. I'd come under my own steam. Driven in fact forty miles (and not in a Reliant Robin). But to be honest only by dint of a few cheery waves and a happy smile had avoided two potential road-rage incidents. Parked nicely (in two and a half tries) with no dents or scratches.

What more do you want?

What use is it to try to justify oneself? Only God can justify and there's no justice in this world, is there? It loves only winners.

Have you ever watched those grand prix winners standing on their podia, wearing million-dollar smiles and baseball caps, squirting gallons of expensive champers over everybody in range, while the world laughs and applauds?

I do pretty much the same thing at a fraction of the cost in a hospital ward and become a *persona non grata*. Why? Because they're winners, and I'm a loser.

Paradoxically, this seemingly negative attitude can have a positive outcome. The taxman is not the only one who wants a self-assessment. God does too.

Faith is born of a need, and it's only when we recognise our need, convince ourselves (with a heartfelt conviction) that only the Divine Physician can put us to rights, that we can come in faith to God.

' *"It is not the healthy who need a doctor, but the sick. . . . I have not come to call the righteous, but sinners."* '
(Matthew 9:12, 13, NIV.)

In this life winners and losers are all the same to God. There is no difference, for all have sinned and fall short of the glory of God (Romans 3:23).

The incredibly beautiful thing about God's love is that it embraces us all. That despite the fact that we are all helpless, inherent losers, it is his express wish that everyone should be a winner. That all should be worthy to receive a gold medal or a crown that will endure for ever and ever.

I can laugh now about my minor disaster, about myself, for *I* don't really matter any more. Self-centredness must go the way of all froth. Evaporation.

I chuckle now when I think of the nurse who wanted to see the back of me.

In retrospect, I see that her words were a joke – and an old-standing joke at that. If I'd only dared to look at her, I would not have seen a basilisk with a lethal stare, but a friendly human, engaged in a little good-natured teasing.

She'd made a point, which reminds me that Jesus Christ never repels anyone. ' *"Whoever comes to me I will never drive away."* ' (John 6:37, NIV.)

A long time ago now, I asked him for help. I was sick. I needed him and no other. And do you know what he said? Quite clearly and quite quietly:

'Welcome, I've been dying to meet you.'

What's in a name?

Are names tyrannical? Are you happy with your name, or has it imposed on you an arbitrary character that you don't really possess?

I admit; I'm not too happy with my second name: Herbert. I have heard some people say: 'He's a bit of a Herbert', yet thankfully I'm not in the same league as a Wally, and why such a noble name as Wallace should be ridiculed, I don't know. In fact I'm rather fond of Wallace *and* Gromit.

Come to think of it, my first name, Tony, has given me a lot of trouble. Mam didn't want Anthony, so my birth certificate has Tony on it. Nobody believes me. I get so many letters to A. Spearing that I'm driven to distraction.

And why do we always want to shorten names? You'd think Tony was short enough, wouldn't you? Although I can't say I've really objected to being called 'Tone', it has set me up as a butt for good-natured teasing.

I've created many a tone *poem* in my time, and been described as a *half* tone by my art colleagues and *semi*-tone by my music-loving acquaintances. The best was when a friend suddenly seemed oblivious to everything I said.

'What *is* the matter with you today?' I queried at last.

'Sorry,' he said. 'I must be getting tone deaf!'

When I was young, forenames were called Christian names. A term our multi-racial society no longer uses. Understandably, because Muslims, Hindus, Buddhists or Jews wouldn't want a 'christian' name, a name given to some Christians at infancy at a christening.

Terry Waite relates a lovely story of a gruff, no-nonsense Suffolk clergyman about to christen a baby girl over a font.

'Name this child,' demanded the reverend.

'Lucy, sir,' came the timid, almost inaudible response.
'WHAT?' thundered the vicar.
'Lucy, sir!' (Fractionally louder.)
'LUCIFER!' cried the cleric. 'That's no name for a boy.
Call him JOHN!' I don't know how Lucy's parents coped;
perhaps they called her Joanna.

We're stuck with our names. Without them we're *non-*persons. We don't exist.

Lionel Blue, well-known *Thought-for-the-day* broadcaster
and writer of really funny books, appeals to my sense of
humour. Here's one of my favourite (most unlikely)
stories, and of course it's appropriately thematic.

There was a Jewish guy who saw a
Far-Eastern gentleman in a city
restaurant. He was out of
sorts, so he picked up a
plate of noodles (as
one does when one
feels like that) and
poured it over the
Chinese gentleman.

'That's for Pearl
Harbour,' he said.

'But I'm Chinese,
not Japanese,' said the
Oriental.

'Chinese, Siamese,
Japanese, what's in a
name?' said the Jew.
As he went to pay
his bill, the Chinese
gentleman hit the
Jewish guy over
the head with a
salami. 'That,' he

said courteously, 'is for sinking the *Titanic*.'

'But,' shouted the Jew, 'the *Titanic* was sunk by an iceberg!'

'Greenberg, Goldberg, iceberg, what's in a name?'

Name-dropping is a curious practice. We use shortened versions, too, or nicknames, suggesting that we number the privileged few as close friends.

I grew up with etiquette (now outmoded) that required polite respect. Mr, Mrs, or Miss prefixed all surnames. Apart from family and friends, of course.

But today? The telephone is frequently used by double-glazing sales persons. And even when a silky-voiced female

latches on to calling me 'Tony', it gets my back up. They're only trying to soften me up for a sale!

My GP calls me 'Tony' too, but I know why. To diagnose my ailments he needs to put me at my ease and ask intimate details. I can't use *his* first name because his profession places a respectful barrier between us. One I would never wish to cross, unless we agreed to become personal friends.

God offers the hand of friendship to all of us, even when we're *un*friendly. He wants everyone to join his family. Invites all to accept Jesus as Saviour.

If we can accept his invitation to share his life with our own, a life that was begotten (not made), then we become sons and daughters of God.

The apostles Paul says: *'And because ye are sons, God hath sent forth the Spirit of his Son into your hearts, crying, Abba, Father.'* (Galatians 4:6, KJV.)

That, to me, expresses an unquestioning trust of intimate affection. Not just tying a creature to its Creator, but an infrangible bond of paternal love.

The Scottish theologian Dr William Barclay asserted that the Aramaic word *Abba* means *Daddy.* And I'm so happy to accept his scholarly insight.

Our Lord said in Matthew 18:3 that: *'Unless you change and become like little children, you will never enter the kingdom of heaven.'* (NIV.)

Little children have their own name for their 'Daddy'. It epitomises that early dependent relationship that, sadly, can be diluted later on in life.

To change means to cause to turn. So why shouldn't we 'turn back', and again become as little children? If it makes it easier to cry 'Abba! – surely one of the loveliest of names – then my earnest supplication is:

'Please, God, make me little again – at least spiritually!'

'For the entrance is low: we must stoop till we are no taller than children in order to get in.' C. S. Lewis.

G-force!

I should imagine that there's hardly ever been a father who's never gone through the agonies of G-force. Mums, too, of course – even more so.

Now I'm certainly not referring to those grotesque, misshapen 'phizogs' of test pilots and astronauts caught on camera, as they undergo that painful freeing of the body from Earth's gravitational pull.

Although as far as I'm concerned it may feel physical, yet it's not. It's our own parental, metaphorical hearts that suffer from this G-force. Emotionally pulled in all directions. Presumably because mums and dads have those selfsame 'cords', those 'ties of love' that God mentions in Hosea 11:4.

Often enough it's sooner rather than later that kids go off into orbit. Trying to free themselves from restraint; the influential, parental pull.

Can we blame them? I can't. I did the same.

'You don't understand, Dad. It's a completely different world from the one you grew up in.'

But why a G-force? Easy!

A Generation Gap that gets ever wider as centuries roll by. It forces children and parents apart. And if those bungee-rope-like ties were never firmly secured in the first place with love – we'd lose them altogether!

It occurs to me that perhaps God was the first to suffer from 'G-force'.

The Bible doesn't tell us how old Adam and Eve were when they initially hid from God in the garden.

Yet we know that Satan, that sneaky serpent, had already encouraged Eve to flex those fledgling flight muscles. With a plan no doubt. Flee the Edenic nest. Gain fallacious 'freedom' from God's so-called 'domination'.

A deceptive concept that promised equality with God and the assurance that: 'You will not surely die.' Failing to stress the inaudible, behind-the-hand, small-print whisper, 'Not immediately, anyway!'

I've puzzled about that question posed to our first parents in Genesis 3:9.

'Where are you?'

We know that God is omniscient and omnipresent so why did he have to ask?

The only conclusion I can glean is that God's questions to men do not always require an answer. They're *giving* an answer.

We know already that he knows, and by asking us, he makes sure we do.

Thus came about that horrendous hiatus of Grand Canyonesque proportions. An immense rift that needed a mountain mover. A gap which could be bridged only by a seismic, supernal Saviour.

When Eve became the Mother of All she carried on the tradition. She bequeathed us a G_3 force.

A Genetically endowed Generation Gap.

How many sons and daughters since then have yelled across that chasm: 'Sorry, Mum. Sorry, Dad. We know better than you do!'

At least they're sorry and we're sorry too, of course. And that's a good new beginning for all of us.

' *"But while he was still a long way off, his father saw him and was filled with compassion for him; he ran to his son, threw his arms around him and kissed him."* '

(Luke 15:20, NIV.)

Fantastic FREE offer!
Too good to miss!

Just before Christmas a neighbour asked my wife and me whether we would be celebrating. I was stunned for a moment. The person concerned knew we were Christians, so why ask?

Later on that same day my son sent me an email: 'Blessed is the season which engages the whole world in a conspiracy of love.' Hamilton Wright Mabie.

Now how should I view that? Cynically or thankfully? Commercialism has eclipsed even that brilliant eastern star of 'exceeding joy'.

Half a century has gone by since John Betjeman wrote of:
The sweet and silly Christmas things,
Bath salts and inexpensive scent
And hideous tie so kindly meant –
supplanted now by more expensive fripperies: DVDs and mobiles.

The first Christmas angel's message was:
'Fear not.
I bring you
good tidings
of great joy,
which shall
be to all people.'
Why has the advent of our Saviour degenerated into an orgy of giving and receiving?

An excuse, a pretext to carouse and feast?

Nevertheless we still, by and large, love Christmas. The spine-tingling magic of 'carolling in frosty air' and the wonderment in a child's shining face.

January Sales inexplicably follow this spending spree. Bombarding us with 'too-good-to-miss, unrepeatable offers'. End of season – Closing-Down Sale!

Thankfully, God does repeat his offer, every Christmas. Every *day*, whenever he can prompt someone to do it. Yet it's only repeatable for as long as life lasts, which, like the world, has only a limited season!

Have no doubts. The Gospel message is the most 'fantastic offer' we'll ever come across in this life. It may seem too good to be true, but it *is* true! God says so and his love not only confirms it in our lives, but also makes it a reality, effective from this very moment.

One of the most dramatic examples of instant salvation was when the thief on the cross recognised Jesus as the Son of God (Luke 23:39-42). Admitting that he deserved punishment, confessing his own unworthiness, he nevertheless was bold enough to ask his Lord

for salvation. There were no conditions, no means testing, not even, 'Have you kept the commandments?' Just a pure, unequivocal, 'Yes.' Granted there and then. Instantly effective!

Who can resist a bargain? Very many, it seems, when it comes to God's unbeatable offer. Live for ever without spending a penny! Why refuse?

It's an offer not subject to status either. God welcomes the self-deficients *and* the self-sufficients. Although if you're among the latter, prepare for some gentle shock therapy! For there *is* a price. We give ourselves.

> *'It is more blessed to give than to receive . . . but the gift of God is eternal life.'*
>
> (Acts 20:35; Romans 6:23.)

No DIYers,
thank you

James Stolz has a dream that he is standing before God on Judgement Day.

'Name?'

'Surely you know me, Lord.'

'Pardon?'

'No need of it, Sir.'

'Look, *I* know your name. *I* know everything about you. But do *you* know who you are?'

'Without a doubt!'

'Kept all the commandments?'
'Of course.'
'What about the eleventh?'
'Every single neighbour I could find!'
'No evil thoughts?'
'How could I? Perish the thought!'
'Are you pleased with your past life?'
'If I *must* be truthful – Yes.'
'Proud?'
'O Lord, could anyone *not* be proud of what I've achieved?'
'Application refused!'
'But, why, Lord? On what grounds?'
'I AM the only perfection. The very fact that you are proud enough to think that you can equal, or even add to my perfection is damning evidence that my grace is spurned. A complete denial of my sacrifice. You, who have tried to be justified by the law, have alienated yourself from me. Condemned yourself by your own imperfect righteousness. Stultified my death on the Cross! Which, sadly, now places you beyond my mercy. Mine is the only name under heaven whereby man can be saved. NEXT!'

James woke up with a start. Rushed off after breakfast and got a deed poll to change his name. No one ever pronounced it properly, and, anyway, he no longer wanted a German name that meant *Pride*. What should he have?

He wanted a name he could live up to and live down to at the same time. A witnessing, talking-point name. A daily-reminder name. He disliked double-barrelled names, yet the one he wanted was triple! Without any doubt there was only one choice.

James No-Other-Name.

'For there is no other name under heaven given to men by which we must be saved.' (Acts 4:12, NIV.)

Blind Date

To be quite honest I've never really liked the TV show *Blind Date*. Yet whenever it was on I found it compulsive viewing. I suppose it was a cleverly contrived trap of audience participation. A snare into which I easily fell.

Not that I could even consider myself remotely eligible to become a contender for the favours of one of those 'gorgeous' girls. I'm far too long in the tooth. Besides, I've been happily married for nearly half a century.

That's not to say, however, that I can't try my hand at being an amateur psychologist. Most of us enjoy observing people. It's a way of whiling away the tedium of waiting at airports, supermarket checkouts and doctors' surgeries.

Perhaps the secret of *Blind Date* as a successful, popular programme was that we, the viewers, had that doubtful advantage of being able to see what everyone looked like. We could judge by appearances. The contestants couldn't. There's no denying that in a boy-meets-girl situation physical attraction plays a vital role. Could that be the strange, obscure reason why even on a blind date, the females are over-dressed or (more than likely) 'under-dressed'?

One of the most frequently heard clichés on the programme was that he (or she) was 'not my type', and colloquially

we say that there's got to be 'chemistry' between two people before any meaningful interaction can evolve. But who knows whether that chemistry will be activated solely by physical attraction or by the meeting of two minds? Maybe it's neither, but a third, mysterious, indefinable 'something'.

For those *Blind Date* contenders it was at first only a meeting of minds. There was a degree of anonymity, screened off as they were from their questioner, which made them far less self-conscious. How else can you account for the daring innuendoes that were bandied around? Would they be said face to face?

Today, the computer has broadened the horizons of countless lonely hearts. Chat-line friendships can be built up from opposite ends of the Earth without either partner having seen the other. These friendships can sometimes stand the litmus paper test of exchanging photographs, but, sadly, not often.

I think that's what I disliked about *Blind Date* – its sadness. One watched the paired-off couple, hand in hand, smiling, almost skipping along to their holiday romance – only to turn up the following week sad and disillusioned. Disappointed, just as the previous week's hopefuls had been. That chemistry was lacking, or we discovered (accompanied by a long-drawn-out 'ahhhhhhh' from the studio audience) it was a case of unrequited love. I never saw even the potential for a happy-ever-after ending.

It occurs to me that God's love affair with the world (John 3:16), and his love affair with you and me in particular, is the only love affair worthy of any compulsive viewing. For it's the only relationship that will have any permanence. To trust and love our Saviour is to ensure that we'll be happy ever after. Literally *ever* after. Forever!

Strangely enough, God makes it a 'blind date', too. He ignores the intellect, the physical, and tells us that *'The Lord does not look at the things man looks at. Man looks at the outward appearance, but the Lord looks at the heart.'*
(1 Samuel 16:7.)

No religion!

'Art, like morality,' says G. K. Chesterton, 'consists in drawing the line somewhere.' Now I'd learned how to draw a line in art school, and eventually became a magazine layout artist. But during my forty-year-long career I must have had difficulty in knowing *where* to draw my lines, for I ended up working on seven different publications.

A good analogy to describe what a layout artist does is to compare it with laying out food on a plate. The more attractive it is, the more likely you are to stimulate appetite. Not that everything I laid out was to my taste. Often I would consider it unpalatable, unwholesome, in fact. After becoming a Christian I looked for a magazine that had relatively good moral standards.

At last I found one, or, to be honest, it found me. The staff of the magazine, about fifty all told, were predominantly women, and most of the men (a mere half a dozen) were on the art side. The ladies with whom I worked represented (in most cases) the very large readership. A loyal million or so who like knitting, home-decorating, and love romantic fiction.

I can only remember one unpleasant, acrimonious argument on religion during the whole of my twenty years there – and that was with the men, incidentally. It was around 1985, about the time a certain North Country bishop was casting doubts on the virgin birth and the resurrection. Sadly, our contentious debate proved to be an unmitigated disaster as far as I was concerned. I ended up feeling emotionally drained, defeated. I wanted to cry on God's shoulder. Arguments on faith seem futile.

Apart from that, however, my job was stressful and my health did suffer. I was therefore 'eased to one side', relieved of responsibility, and as compensation asked to do a little writing and illustrating.

One day I was overjoyed to be commissioned by my editor to produce an illustrated article on Easter. But there was one proviso:

'Tone,' she peremptorily ordered. '*No* religion!'

I was about to remonstrate, but I knew I could easily lose the whole project. What she really meant was – no doctrinal theology.

Modesty to the winds – it turned out fairly well and hardly a jot or tittle was altered. After the Easter weekend a colleague greeted me with, 'Did you listen to BBC Radio 4 on Saturday morning? Your article was mentioned. I didn't hear all that was said – but it was complimentary.'

Our Press Relations department got hold of the following transcript when guest reviewer Mary Kenny was reviewing weekly publications;

Mary Kenny: 'Obviously the religious weeklies do mark Easter, as does the modest *Woman's Weekly* in a sweet and well-informed piece on Easter traditions, ending on the hosanna that:

Reader: 'CHRIST IS RISEN!'

Mary Kenny: 'Better not tell the Bishop of Durham!'

God had turned defeat into victory.

Not only had one million or so readers had the chance to read about that cornerstone of our faith – *'If Christ has not been raised, our preaching is useless and so is your faith'* (1 Corinthians 15:14, NIV), but at least another (estimated) four million radio listeners had heard about it too.

'So shall my word . . . accomplish that which I please.' (Isaiah 55:11.)

No part-exchange

'For if a man is in Christ he becomes a new person altogether – the past is finished and gone, everything has become fresh and new.' (2 Corinthians 5:17, JBP.)

' "If anyone loves me, he will obey my teaching. My Father will love him, and we will come to him and make our home with him." ' (John 14:23, NIV.)

One of the most important decisions in life is buying a new car, and, in an odd way, it does have strong similarities to *the* most important decision in life.

Mr B takes delivery of a brand-new model. He's so excited he can't sleep. Lies awake worrying about it, uneasy about certain aspects of the deal. Next morning at the showroom he meets Paul who seems very knowledgeable.

'About my old car,' says Mr B. 'How much am I allowed part exchange?'

'Nothing!' Paul replies.

'B-b-but,' Mr B stammers, 'I know it wasn't in marvellous condition. Mileage a bit high . . . um . . . Surely I could have the radio-cassette back?'

'Sorry; it's gone!'

'Gone? Where?'

Paul shrugs. 'Bottom of the sea. Forget it. It's gone. Buried!'

Mr B's voice is a little hoarse now. 'Does that mean,' he rasps, 'that I'll have to pay the full whack – the whole price?'

'No,' says Paul firmly.

A sigh of relief, but still anxious. 'How much a month then? Say over five years. I suppose I could manage that with overtime and extra work.'

Paul smiles. 'Look; there's nothing to pay.'

Mr B is bewildered. There *must* be a catch somewhere. 'What about insurance then? The premiums on a model like this could be prohibitive!'

'No insurance necessary.'

'Nonsense!' Mr B almost explodes. 'Ridiculous! What guarantee have . . .'

'*He's* your guarantee.'

'Who is?' asks an incredulous Mr B.

'The Boss.'

Poor Mr B now suspects he won't be the *real* owner. 'How does that work?'

'He comes with you.'

'Oh no!' exclaims Mr B. 'I knew there was a drawback – the trouble I had with the wife's mother – sat in the

back seat, didn't stop. . . .'

'You misunderstand,' says Paul.

'But you said, "He's coming." '

'Right!' laughs Paul, 'and the Father too.'

'How on earth?'

'Look,' Paul tries to explain, 'This is the most advanced model you'll ever get. They won't be with you in the physical sense, but they'll guide, talk to you – as long as you'll listen. They'll even take over completely if you agree.'

'Like a radio . . .' Mr B was groping for words, 'like a remote control – helping with road conditions and speed traps. . . .'

'Got it in one!' says Paul.

'Ah!' Mr B is suddenly worried. 'But if *I'm* driving what happens if I have an accident? It's inevitable on today's roads. Even the best drivers can have a bump.'

'He takes the blame.'

'Even when *I'm* driving?'

'Yes.'

Mr B is stunned. 'It's just too good to be true,' he murmurs.

'For it is by grace that you have been saved, through faith – and this not from yourselves, it is the gift of God.'
(Ephesians 2:8, 9, NIV.)

Fragile – with care

However did we carry eggs before egg-boxes? They might have been around in the late 1940s, yet I can't remember them.

I did not like delivering eggs on my rural milk round. Glass bottles were fragile enough, but eggs! They seemed to break if you *looked* at them!

During the war, 'Monty' (Viscount of Alamein) could well have been the general who popularised the beret. A form of headgear that was most versatile.

Whenever I ran out of paper bags, which was often, I'd use my navy-blue beret as an egg-carrier. With one hand holding two milk bottles and the other clasping a beret full of eggs, I'd attempt to enter a garden gate. I was proud of my skill. Latches could be tricky, and a spring-loaded gate called for a deft half-pirouette on one foot while the other kicked it open.

Pride was due for a fall. One day I tackled a gate-spring of such spiteful velocity that I was almost knocked over. My beret caught the impact and UGH! A gooey mess! What do you do with a beret full of broken eggs?

My father once kept chickens and built a neat little hen house. He was told that solid china eggs would encourage hens to lay, so he bought some. The trick was to show visitors the hen house, pick up a china egg and throw it, saying, 'Catch!' Didn't matter if they dropped it. It would almost bounce.

God has created fragile eggs and fragile people – with a few china-egg types thrown in. There are people who 'bounce back', but aren't there more who are easily crushed and end up with their lives in a hopeless mess?

We are beholden, surely, as Christians, to treat one another (everybody) with the greatest of care, with loving gentleness and sensitivity. When a stranger comes to church for the first time, realise that the world has most probably handled him very roughly. That person seeks the Divine Physician.

Remember that they could desire to retain their anonymity for a while. 'Lapsed church members', too, often dread returning to church, fearful of being embarrassed with an 'over-the-top' welcome back.

Have you ever put your hand under the breast of a broody hen sitting on her clutch of eggs? It's so soft, so warm, so *lovely.*

If God knows how to look after fragile eggs, he must surely know how to look after his fragile children.

'A bruised reed he shall not break, and the smoking flax shall he not quench.' (Isaiah 42:3, KJV.)

No end to it

One of the most fascinating things about language (for me at least) is that certain words can have a wealth of meaning. And that even a short, three-letter word has the latent power, when understood significantly, of course, to change the whole pattern and direction of life.

The word I have in mind is *end*. It's a Middle English word that has parallels in many other languages. Sanskrit has *anta*, which interestingly enough gives us the prefixes of *ante*, *anti*, and *an*, as in *an*-swer.

The *Concise Oxford Dictionary* has the following as its first entry under *end*: *The extreme limit; the point beyond which a thing does not continue.*

This word seems to have no end to its uses. Come to a bad (or sticky) end. Reach the end of the road. Get such a fright that one's hair stands on end!

My favourite Bible verse with end is: *Christ is the end of the law so that there may be righteousness for everyone who believes.* (Romans 10:4, NIV.)

There are many differing interpretations in other translations.

J. B. Phillips: *For Christ means the end of the struggle for righteousness-by-the-Law for everyone who believes in him.* Good News: *For Christ has brought the Law to an end, so that everyone who believes is put right with God.* New English Bible: *For Christ ends the law and brings right-eousness for everyone who has faith.* And to conclude I also have a German version of *The Good News* which states that the law is no longer the way to God.

Now each of these agrees that everyone who believes is put right with God. Yet isn't there some ambiguity regarding the law? We may wonder what has happened to the law. It can't surely mean that it's come to an *end*.

Perhaps this fogginess is to do with usage. Whether *end* is used as a noun or a verb. When I was in school we were taught that a noun is a name

and a verb is a 'doing' word. The difficulty here is that *to end* won't fit into the category of a 'doing' word. It's more akin to an *un*doing word.

That's not to say that *end* has only a negative, dismal finality. Sometimes after a tedious sermon, when a minister says, 'I end . . .', many of his or her congregation may find it the most joyous word they've heard all morning!

And Romans 10:4 *is* a joy to all believers. Christ is the *doing* of our *un*doing.

Not because the Law's abrogated, zapped to the recycle bin. NO WAY! It's been fulfilled. Is being fulfilled now! On our behalf by our dear Redeemer.

Guilt is a poison that perniciously pervades our body, mind and soul. It not only ruins our health but our relationship with God. He and only he can detoxify us from the dark power of this lethal poison. *'He rescued us from the power of darkness and brought us safe into the kingdom of his dear Son, by whom we are set free, that is, our sins are forgiven.'* (Colossians 1:13, 14, GNB.)

Free now from the dreaded condemnation of the Law (Romans 8:1). Free now to use fulfilling belief. A New (God-serving) Life, living 'in' his perfect law-keeping. Don't harbour any of sin's antagonism against the Law. For the Law is as much a part of God as is his love. Christ gives us the green light to dare to believe what we never dared we *could* believe.

Living not at one's own risk. But at God's (ie no risk at all).

We live now under grace. No longer under the Law but with the Law. In other words – *with* Jesus Christ. Following the promptings of his Spirit.

'For sin pays its wage – death; but God's free gift is eternal life in union with Christ Jesus our Lord.' (Romans 6:23, GNB.)

Three sixteen
The twenty-six words of life

The radio programme 'Desert Island Discs' has been running for a very long time. It's still considered an accolade to be chosen as an interviewee, to be asked to make your choice of favourite records. And if you are chosen, the inference is that you're someone special.

There's not the remotest possibility that I will ever be chosen. That I will experience those proverbial 'fifteen minutes of fame' that most people seem to clamour for. Yet I would like to pretend that I have been invited to participate. Not to choose my favourite music (although I love music dearly) but for the choice that is tucked away right at the end of the programme.

Each candidate is asked: 'What book, apart from the Bible and the Complete Works of Shakespeare, would you like to take with you to read on your desert island?'

I've pondered on this for a long time, and finally come up with the following question-cum-answer: 'Will the

rules allow me to have not a book but a complete orchestral score of a Haydn symphony?'

Of course somebody is bound to ask why have the score when you can listen to the disc? Ah! But as I'm already (at my time of life) getting hard of hearing, if I do become totally deaf, I can 'hear' it, so to speak, in my 'mind's ear'. Some bright spark may add – if your faculties are now in such a parlous state, who's to know whether you might go blind as well. What then?

I'm prepared for that one. As a contingency measure, I'd ask for the luxury of my favourite Bible verse cut into a slab of polished granite. I could then every day, as long as I lived, run my fingers over those lovely words.

Which verse would I choose? There's a myriad to choose from, I know. Yet it's no problem for me. There is only one verse, to my mind, that sums up the gospel message and reveals that priceless jewel of God's grace. A verse that quotes the very words of Jesus himself and can be found in John 3:16.

The twenty-six words of life

' *"For God so loved the world that he gave his one and only Son, that whoever believes in him shall not perish but have eternal life."* ' (NIV.)

Would I need to be reminded of it? Day in, day out? Perhaps not. I feel it's written on my heart. Yet I'd want that verse to be left there on that desert island. Hurricanes, tidal waves, volcanic eruptions could well destroy, wash away my Bible, gramophone, discs, etc. In years to come, when I am no longer, my slab of granite would hopefully still be a witness to God's love.

An invitation to Heaven.

Have you noticed how numbers have a significance in language?

The greatest number landmark in our modern world is now Nine Eleven.

How I long for the day when it could be Three Sixteen!

Only once?

'You're only young once.'

This is usually a tolerant remark made by older members of the human race to excuse the wild extravagances of younger (not yet paid up) members of the human race.

Nobody ever seems to say, 'Ah, and you're only *old* once too!' Because obviously it's not the case. As far as I'm concerned I frequently feel that I'm old once too often!

I find that I've been old for a long time. An insufferably long time.

Perhaps it was because I longed for retirement long before I was ready for it. I'd never realised how good it was to do

work that was appreciated. Do something purposeful and fulfilling. Enjoy the consolation of a reward for earning my living.

'A man can do nothing better than to eat and drink and find satisfaction in his work. This too, I see, is from the hand of God, for without him, who can eat or find enjoyment.'
(Ecclesiastes 2:24, 25, NIV.)

Hobbies are okay. Gardening, grass cutting and, of course, DIY (but liable to SOS crises).

Our house was like painting the Forth Bridge. It now has a new plastic coat which, as they say, 'should see me out'.

Solomon puts it so aptly: *'Better one handful with tranquillity than two handfuls with toil.'*
(Ecclesiastes 4:6, NIV.)

But with two hands (and feet) I took up playing the church organ. It was hard (for me at least). My feet wouldn't co-operate. Presumably because I'd put them in it once too often. They had a (prematurely aged) will of their own. Performing *their* (not *my*) voluntaries. The rest of me, thankfully, *was* remaining in my relatively young sixties!

A minister friend invited me to play at a little church in Derbyshire to celebrate its centenary.

There was a lovely old organ with a mellow, sonorous tone and no pedals. Super to play!

Local press representatives turned up and interest was shown in one of the members, who was a centenarian. He, as yet, hadn't arrived but had promised to perform his favourite hymn on the organ.

Meanwhile I busied myself in opening up the instrument and sorting the music. I was taken aback, however, when a sidesman doling out hymnbooks asked me if *I* was 'the hundred-year-old organist'!

I secretly bought some anti-wrinkle cream on the way home.

Our venerable VIP turned up and clarified confusion, for the minister and I had literally to lift him onto the organ bench.

'I have made you and I will carry you,' God promises the old and grey-haired (Isaiah 46:4, NIV). The future bodes bright at least.

Of course I'm not alone in trying to come to terms with the *'scrap-heap* mentality' that besets many 'before-their-time' pensioners.

But does God have an answer?

I believe he does.

'Whatever you do, work at it with all your heart, as working for the Lord, not for men, since you know that you will receive an inheritance from the Lord as a reward. It is the Lord Christ you are serving.' (Colossians 3:23, 24, NIV.)

I give up!

John chapter 6 verse 44 tells us that no one can come to
Jesus unless the Father, who sent him, draws him. Now
what is this drawing? Is it a magnetic attraction? Maybe we
could call it a 'compulsion of love'. One thing we can be
sure; it's not an involuntary compulsion. We are not
inexorably sucked into God's love like
helpless ants into a
vacuum cleaner!

God in his
wisdom
gave us

free will. I believe it was Martin Luther who inferred that he didn't want it! Whether we want it or not, it's there. The best thing to do is willingly pay homage to God's will so that our will is in harmony with his. Assuring us that anything we ask, he will hear (1 John 5:14).

So what is God's will for us? I think it's his dearest wish that we should feed on the Bread which came down from heaven (John 6:58) – have that lost divine image restored in us. He who eats this Bread lives for ever. Our Father in Heaven made this restoration possible. For again we find that God (as J. B. Phillips has it) *puts it into our hearts* to come to our Saviour. He, only he, has the words of eternal life (John 6:65).

Why do we hesitate? Perhaps *you* don't. But I do. Am I ego-centrically orientated? Is the only pivotal figure in my life *me*?

' "*If anyone would come after me, he must deny himself and take up his cross and follow me.*" '
(Matthew 16:24, NIV.)

Deny himself. That's clear enough. *Self*-denial. We follow a Servant King. One whose whole life was one of self-sacrifice. It's a Christian's loving duty to think or care more for others than he does of himself. *Love your neighbour as yourself.*

Our hearts warm to the thought that this

word, love, is *agape*: God's love. Show this love in our lives
and we reveal God in us – for God *is* love!

But going back to Matthew 16:24. Why do we need to
take up our cross?

Many people have the idea that the cross each Christian
has to bear symbolises the trials and hardships of life. The
writer Jack Sequeira believes this to be a mistaken idea. I
think he's right.

For aren't *all* people the target for the 'slings and arrows
of outrageous fortune'? Atheists and agnostics, unbelievers
and believers – 'don't knows' – all suffer the consequences
of living in a sin-ravaged world. True, we'll be persecuted,
suffer for our faith, but I feel that's not the implication here.

There is only one cross in the life of a Christian, the cross
on which the Saviour of the world was crucified. So surely
the cross which Jesus calls us to bear must be his cross and
no other.

Nevertheless, there's no denying that Jesus does say that
if anyone would follow him he or she must take up his or
her cross. A personal cross.

When there were divisions in the church at Corinth, Paul
asked (1 Corinthians 1:13): *'Was Paul crucified for you?'*
and then in his letter to the Galatians (2:20 and 6:14) he
admitted that he had *'been crucified with Christ'*, and trusted
that he (Paul) might *'never boast except in the cross of our
Lord Jesus'*.

Is there a contradiction here? Are there *two* crosses for a
Christian? I don't think so. I believe there's an added dimen-
sion to the one cross of Calvary.

We sing in *'The Old Rugged Cross'* that it's an 'emblem of
suffering and shame'. Isn't it also a symbol of self-sacrifice?
Morris Venden in his book *To Know God* (pages 39, 40)
gives us this explanation:

'The cross is used in scripture as a symbol of surrender,
death to self. Jesus spoke of our cross. He invites us to take

up our cross and follow him. He uses the cross, the cruci-
fixion, as a symbol to teach us that we cannot surrender
ourselves; we must allow God to do the work for us.'

Christ is my personal Saviour. My inherent sinful nature
died with him on the cross (Romans 6:6). If I can say with
all my heart, as Paul did, *'I have been crucified with Christ,'*
and *'through his blood, shed on the cross for me'* I am now
reconciled to God himself – then to my mind that makes
the cross my personal symbol. My symbol of re-creation,
restoration and reconciliation!

But how does all this happen? How can I? Paul tells the
Ephesians, *'Put off your old self . . . and put on the new self,*
created to be like God in true righteousness and holiness.'
(4:22, 24, NIV)

Morris Venden points out that you cannot crucify yourself. Someone else must do it.

It goes without saying, I'm sure, that this conception of
being crucified is metaphorical, yet Christ's death was a
reality. Christ's death was a voluntary submission. Likewise,
my death to self must be a reality, a voluntary submission to
God. Only he can rid me of my tiresome, sinful, selfish self.

Wanting to surrender is the
first step. It's not a forced
capitulation to an enemy.
It's a freewill act. The
handing over of my life
to a friend. A friend
who has already given
his life for me and you.
Surely the *only* reciprocal
response we *can* give.

A reaction to the silent
demands of a love that
expects nothing – yet
hopes for everything.

Better than we ever dreamed

'Tony,' said a voice on the phone, 'can you do us a large painting of our new factory?'

'I might be able to,' I replied, cautiously. 'Where is it?'

'Nowhere at the moment. It's only an architect's plan.'

'Send it to me,' I said boldly. 'I'll let you know.'

My mind was buzzing. How do you work out the perspective from a flat, one-dimensional drawing? They wanted an elevated viewpoint too, and those roof angles were most unusual. I'd better play safe and refuse.

Inspiration for me usually comes with the dawn chorus. And just after my favourite blackbird's second deep-throated warble, I got it.

I'd make a small cardboard model from cereal boxes, and draw it from that.

After I was given the colour of the bricks, roof tiles, etc, it began to take shape. I added flowerbeds, trees and shrubs and the end result was better than I dared hope. Everybody seemed happy. Some kind person said it was 'far better than we ever dreamed it would be'. How nice!

The acid test of course came months later when the factory was finally built, but my 'impression' was remarkably like the real thing. No one was more surprised than I was.

Talking of 'impressions', I once wrote a magazine article on the French impressionist painter Renoir, tying up with the opening of a big London exhibition. I'd spent weeks immersing myself in as many reproductions of his pictures as I could find. But nothing could prepare me for the impact of seeing his *original* paintings for the first time. I was bowled over by the vibrancy of his colours. As alive as if they'd been painted the day before.

Is it futile to indulge, luxuriate on the joyful anticipation of Heaven, when it is, as yet, unseen? We have only an outline plan, few details and a vague impression at the very least. Speculation can run riot, but none of us will really know what it's like until we get there.

Sadly, some are warily apprehensive. I've heard questions such as: 'Will our pets be there?' I know of a widow, married to a second husband, who is troubled about what to say to her first when they meet up again in Heaven.

I asked a minister how he coped with such queries.

'Heaven will be far better than we ever dreamed it would be,' he said. 'Out of this world! No problems! We'll love it because Jesus will be there.'

Rejoice and be exceedingly glad. It's going to be great.

'Our light and momentary troubles are achieving for us an eternal glory that far outweighs them all. So we fix our eyes not on what is seen, but on what is unseen.' (2 Corinthians 4:17, 18, NIV.)

All change!
Can a leopard change his spots?

When Groucho Marx, the famous comedian, heard that a friend had been denied membership to an exclusive golf club because of racial prejudice, he quipped the following response, 'Quite right too! I wouldn't want to belong to a club that allows the likes of me to be a member!'

Now maybe that's just a laugh at his own expense, or maybe it's genuine humility. But are we willing to recognise ourselves as we really are? Do we recognise our need to change?

When I left hospital after a triple heart bypass, I was given a booklet listing the dos and don'ts for a patient recovering from open-heart surgery. It stated too that a person like me would be difficult to live with for at least a year.

My wife smiled rather wistfully when she heard that.

'But you always have been,' she said.

I know I'm not the nicest of persons – touchy, over-sensitive, bad-tempered, *very* prickly, especially a.m. But what can I do to change myself?

Nothing. It's impossible!

The sobering truth is that *I* do not have the power to change myself. Only God has that power. ' *"With man this is impossible, but with God all things are possible."* ' (Matthew 19:26.)

We know that God loves us just as we are. Yet won't that lead to complacency? He doesn't want us to love ourselves just as we are. He wants us to love *him* so much that we're dissatisfied with ourselves!

He longs for *us* to be like him – and no other. He is the only role model.

He invites *us* to share his life (Revelation 3:20)!

And only we can let him in.

'As soon as Jesus was baptised, he went up out of the water. At that moment heaven was opened, and he saw the Spirit of God descending like a dove and lighting on him. And a voice from heaven said, "This is my Son, whom I love; with him I am well pleased." ' (Matthew 3:16, 17, NIV.)

Balm from Harrods

Jenny kissed me when we met,
Jumping from the chair she sat in . . .

There is much that I don't understand in Leigh Hunt's short poem, but I do recognise a consolation when I see one. When the going was rough, Jenny's kiss was a consolation.

Sidonie didn't kiss me. Nothing like that! Didn't even jump from a chair. She walked across the school hall and spoke to me – only a short sentence, graced with a smile. I was in my twenties; she at least thirty years older. But forty years hence those words were still a balm of consolation.

The school was the venue for our operatic society's rehearsals. I was 'hon. accompanist at rehearsals only', which precluded me from the old theatre pit that was hardly big enough for the *ad hoc* collection of musicians who made up the orchestra. We were at the end of months of rehearsals, and as I got up from the piano I noticed her coming. I'd never seen her before.

'Your playing was a pleasure to listen to,' she said. That was all.

Later I asked our musical director, 'Who was she?'

'You *must* know *her*!' he replied impatiently. 'That's Sidonie Goossens – principal harpist for the BBC Symphony Orchestra. Such luck getting her in the orchestra!'

My musical dictionary has nearly a column devoted to the Goossens family, all illustrious musicians. So my balm was top quality – only stocked at Harrods. But why did I cherish this particular brand? Because I've always believed that music should carry a *Health Warning*.

High on the list of ingredients for good music is heartfelt emotion. That's why music makers are so easily hurt and bruised by unkind comments.

One summer's evening many decades later I switched on to Radio Three and there was Richard Baker's familiar voice.

'Earlier,' he reported, 'promenaders gave a rapturous, affectionate welcome to Sidonie Goossens – she must be in her nineties!'

Imagination took me to the Albert Hall. If I'd had the temerity to approach her, what would have happened? Suddenly my illusions were shattered. She couldn't possibly have remembered me! And let's be honest, weren't her words nothing more than a well-bred, polite reaction?

The balm had lost is fragrance, well past its 'best before' date.

Sorry, Sidonie, but I've got a better consolation now. He didn't cross the school hall, jump from a chair. He ran a million miles just to tell me something. When the going's rough, he it is who comes, puts his arm around my shoulders and whispers: 'Don't worry; it *will* pass. I know exactly how you feel.'

Thank you, Jenny. Thank you, Sidonie.

But above all – Thank you, my Lord Jesus. For giving me, for giving us, your everlasting consolation.

(2Thessalonians 2:16, KJV).

Moaning Minnie

When World War Two broke out I was just ten years old. Obviously that's a fair while ago now but I still remember a few things quite vividly.

Air raid sirens were tested as fire alarms are today. And it wasn't long before sirens were given the appropriate endearment of 'Moaning Minnie'.

Yet of course no one welcomed the sound, which always produced an icicle of fear in *my* tum at least.

If it was school time most of us were secretly pleased (apart from a few who audibly cheered) as we all trooped out into the corridors to spend an uncomfortable hour or so until the 'all clear' sounded. The more worldly among us had the foresight to bring a pack of cards.

I remember taking my first violin lesson two weeks before the start of the War and I'd hoped that such frivolities would be suspended.

Sadly, no.

The best place to practise was our acoustically sympathetic bathroom. Hardly convenient, for as the bathroom possessed our only toilet it soon became an *in*convenience.

One day while trying to develop my skills with 8v *portamento* (that is, sliding up the scale with one finger) I noticed people, through the open window, scurrying for their end-of-garden shelters.

I gave up, not because I was accused of creating hoax alarms, mainly because my E string had the viciousness of a wire cheese cutter.

No one likes a 'moaner'. I suppose, at least inwardly, I've done my share of bemoaning. I was a pretty (sorry, wrong word) *pathetic*-looking schoolboy. Burdened with a squint and a stammer. The butt of many jokes.

Maybe, just maybe, it was these disadvantages that eventually led me into publishing. Visual (as distinct from vocal) communication, expressing what I felt in pictures, etc, and also the hobby of music, which is really putting into sound what can't be said in words or speech.

Helen Keller was that extraordinary lady who overcame great physical handicaps (being deaf and blind) to become an outstanding communicator. Perhaps not so much *in spite of* her disabilities but *because of* them. Knowing her 'thorn in the flesh', how much more poignant are her words: 'I cried because I had no shoes, until I met someone who had no feet.'

Paul, the apostle, writes to the Corinthians in his second letter (chapter 12) that he was given a sharp pain in his body, which he interprets as Satan's messenger to bruise him. Save him from becoming unduly elated. Paul asks the Lord to rid him of it, yet his answer is:

' *"My grace is all you need; power comes to its full strength in weakness."* '

(Verses 7-9, NEB.)

Whether you or I have weaknesses that can be made into strengths is only for God to decide. He may on occasions supply our wants, but only if they're our needs as well. So what's our trenchant 'thought-for-today'? No more Moaning Minnies, thank you!

Extraterrestrial navigation?

Now and again after I've cracked some witticism or complimented a member of the fairer sex on her youthful appearance, I hear:

'Oh! How lovely. You've made my day!'

It cheers me up too, because by nature I indulge in a lot of self-deprecation. I'm very consciously aware of my faults. Shakespeare's advice? Assume a virtue if you have it not.

Ah! That's all very well. But what if I'm unassuming anyway?

As a Christian I should remind myself daily of God's promise.

'If anyone acknowledges that Jesus is the Son of God, God lives in him and he in God.' (1 John 4:15, NIV.)

Now this is a tricky one. One of those concepts that most people (even Christians) consider intangible. Something they are unable to grasp mentally. Its nearest correlation could be telepathy. And surprisingly enough, many married couples who have been together for a long time do experience uncanny, instantaneous thought duplication.

Science, apparently, denies its existence. But as Father Brown (G. K. Chesterton's priest-cum-sleuth) so wisely said: 'A man of science isn't trying to prove anything. He's trying to find out what will prove itself.'

Bible-based Christians will surely acknowledge that you cannot belong to Christ unless you 'have' the Spirit within you (Romans 8:9). I feel humbly, deep down in my heart, that the Spirit of Christ has been, and is with me, very often. I can't prove it – I can only hope that the Spirit will.

A friend of mine would often know it was me phoning him without my saying a word. In fact, as a stammerer I sometimes *couldn't* say a word. Yet he knew (by some sixth sense, I suppose) that it was me, struggling with a speech block. He'd say, 'Hi, Tone. How're things?' His normality broke the tension.

The unspiritual man cannot make sense of what God wants us to know. His is a wisdom that baffles the human intellect.

Studying a map can be a very interesting pastime. But there's no real point in doing so unless you're going somewhere. Scripture can undoubtedly reveal God, and I, like many others, thought I could find God mentally, just by reading about him.

We need aid. In reality we need an Aide.

The Spirit of God.

Map reading. Bible reading. We need the *Spiritual Cartographer.*

Whenever I plan to drive by car to a large, faraway city, I pore over the latest road maps and make a list of all the routes that I'll need.

But I still get lost!

Satellite Navigation could be the answer. And thereby lies a spiritual application!

Ideally, I'd love someone, someone who has been along that road before, to sit beside me. To guide me through all the traffic problems, the diversions and perhaps even take over when I'm tired and bewildered. Someone I could trust implicitly.

Trust with my life.

I know he is there. Yet, strangely, he doesn't always seem like a 'he', but non-gendered. More like a mother, a sister, a friend or . . .

Just like the constant companion I've always wanted.

The best moment of my day is just before I go to sleep. I send God a knee-mail: 'Thanks, Lord, you've made my day.'

'If the Spirit is the source of our life, let the Spirit direct our course.' (Galatians 5:25, NEB.)

Birthdays

When our children were younger, they all clubbed together and bought me a sandwich-toaster for my birthday. Never in my wildest fantasies had I ever thought of owning one! *They* obviously wanted one, and were hoping that I would too!

To be honest, I was just that little bit disappointed. Yet we did *all* enjoy toasted sandwiches every day for the next month or so, until the novelty wore off and our appetites jaded. But novelties rarely age all that well, do they?

My conscience pricked. Perhaps I was being ungrateful, too focused on self. Birthdays obviously have a tendency to make a chap introvertive, and I was no exception.

As the Duchess says in Alice in Wonderland: 'Everything's got a moral, if only you can find it!' So, what's the moral in all this? I think we may find it if we take a closer look at the word self.

Self is a funny word. On its own fairly respectable, almost

innocuous you might say – and it crops up frequently in everyday language. Pretty harmless until you add 'ish' to it!

'Look after yourself, take care!' is a nice, kind, charitable phrase. Yet if we say to someone: 'Don't get too wrapped up in yourself!' we're sounding a critical note.

A ring of warning.

Praise, Love, Glory, Pity, Righteousness. All good, straightforward, wholesome words. But prefix them with 'self' followed by a hyphen, and what do you get?

A contamination.

Self becomes a pollutant, it makes a good word into an *un*word. Admittedly, it appears to have no power over '*anti*-self' attributes such as, denial, criticism and sacrifice, etc; and many words like, education, discovery and confidence seem to be actually enhanced by being coupled with self. Even lending self a sort of nobility. Elevating it onto a pedestal!

Don't be deceived. Inherent in self is a hidden agenda.

' "*If anyone wishes to be a follower of mine,*" ' said Jesus, ' "*he must leave self behind.*" ' (Matthew 16:24, NEB.)

Now what does this mean? Are we to lose self? In some way forget it? Repudiate or give up all right to one's self? We should know that the man (or woman) we once were has been crucified with Christ (Romans 6:6). So I believe any self that we find ourselves with now must be our new true self, or at least it should be! The spirit-receptive self that it pleases God to renew constantly back to his own, intended image (1 Colossians 3:10, NEB).

Is not 'loving your neighbour as yourself' another way of saying: 'Take as much care and consideration of others as you do of yourself'?

To keep Alice's Duchess happy, what moral can we find, then? Is there a lesson to be learned from the little dilemma I've had when feeling unhappy with my birthday present? Should I confess that I'd have been over the moon with a kilo or so of my favourite, dark plain chocolate instead!

What's my problem?

Is it that self-gratification, self-indulgence, are alien to the Kingdom of God?

Yes, I reluctantly admit that they are. Although some might say (and I'm one of them) 'Isn't that a bit harsh – you try telling that to a child on its birthday?'

Perhaps I'm still a child at heart, for my heart tells me that our Father in Heaven is a bountiful parent, who delights in giving us good things. Showers us with blessings.

How do you feel about the Wisdom of Solomon? Some feel uncomfortable – yet it's still Scripture. This is a quote from the Good News version of Ecclesiastes 9:7: *'Go ahead – eat your food and be happy; drink your wine and be cheerful. It's all right with God.'*

God wants us to enjoy life.

If we don't, our physical and spiritual health will surely suffer. This wisdom, of course, should be balanced with the freedom that God gives us.

In 1 Corinthians 6:12 we read that: 'As a Christian I *may* do anything, but that does not mean that everything is good for me. I may do everything, but I must not be a slave of anything.' (J. B. Phillips.)

Using Paul's guidance again, also from 1 Corinthians, this time 10:24, we find him advising us that no follower of Christ should seek to gain his own advantage, but seek the good of his neighbour.

So the point is, quite simply, that even on our birthdays, especially on our birthdays, we should think more of others than we do of ourselves.

Or better still celebrate a commemoration of our 'born-again birthday' every day!

Road rage

I think road rage is not just a recent phenomenon; it's been with us for some time. More prevalent now, admittedly, than fifty or more years ago when we had far fewer vehicles. My vehicle had two wheels and just one horsepower, or, to be more accurate, a large black pony called Bill. It was a milk float.

Bill and I delivered milk for a small dairy farm situated about a mile down the lane from the village high street.

A good, healthy job as far as jobs go. Apart from having to get up very early, collect money on rainy days – and dogs. Why do dogs have such a strong aversion to postmen and milkmen? Scientists tell us that they're only guarding their territory. But what happened to God's promise to Adam

(Genesis 1:28) that he would rule over every living thing? Most of the four-legged, aggressive lumps of snarling fur I encountered had never heard of it.

Skip lived in a cottage in the High Street. A nondescript dog, not big, not small. The children in the family loved him, were always pulling him about.

Mondays were not my favourite. Most of the Western World enjoys a 'lie in' on Sundays and my little patch of rural Hertfordshire was no exception. Consequently, our return to the dairy on Mondays meant having the float doubly full of empty bottles. Skip invariably chose that time to attack. Not me, but Bill! Like a greyhound he'd streak out of the cottage gate, barking and snapping with frightening ferocity. Bill hated him, and his usual rhythmic trot changed into a jerky half gallop, tumbling loose bottles all over the place.

One such black Monday my hitherto suppressed rage unleashed itself. I grabbed a bottle by its neck and flung it

down at the running dog. To my astonishment it exploded with a loud 'PHUT' on Skip's head. Before we careered round the corner I saw him rolling senseless into a ditch.

Triumphant elation? Yes, but very short-lived. I soon realised that I'd more than likely *killed* a family pet.

While finishing my work at the dairy I argued inwardly, trying to justify my action – yet I couldn't. Remorse soon set in, and I began to feel true repentance and sorrow. How could I make amends? Confess? Buy a new puppy for the children?

After rounding the corner of the lane I got off my bike and peered into the ditch. Nothing there! Had they found him already? Puzzled, I crossed the High Street and there, sunning himself on the front doormat, was Skip! Dazed-looking, but definitely ALIVE! I called him and he cowered in submission.

Laughing with joy, I knew instinctively that he'd never chase Bill again.

He'd learnt a lesson. Had I? I hope so.

'Anger is cruel and fury overwhelming.' (Proverbs 27:4, NIV.)

As we are one

Is it my imagination? Or is there a reticence among Christians, a disposition to silence, when it comes to an acknowledgement that God lives in us?

'For thus saith the high and lofty One that inhabiteth eternity, whose name is Holy; I dwell in the high and holy place, with him also that is of a contrite and humble spirit, to revive the spirit of the humble, and revive the heart of the contrite ones.' (Isaiah 57:15.)

God loves to live in a humble and contrite heart. Yet should we, in our humility combined with shyness, keep quiet about it?

'My soul will boast in the Lord; let the afflicted hear and rejoice. Glorify the Lord with me: let us exalt his name together.' (Psalm 34:2, 3, NIV.)

C. S. Lewis claimed that the whole purpose of becoming Christians is simply nothing else than sharing our lives with the life of Christ, the Son of God. Share a life that was begotten. And being begotten, become sons and daughters of God.

In John's gospel, chapter 17, there's that beautiful prayer of Jesus to the Father, where he not only prays for himself, but for his disciples and all believers, including us. That repetitive theme of oneness impresses me. And I'm sure that our Lord has not repeated this particular request because the Father will not hear the first time round. It must be for our benefit: *' "That they may be one as we are one: I in them and you in me." '* (Verses 22, 23, NIV.)

Atonement is often thought of as a difficult word. Jesus puts it so simply that even a child can understand, 'We're friends now, so let's keep together.'

The Father, the Son, you and I. It's an at-one-ment. In

adult terms, the reconciliation of God and man.

I had the unenviable task, many years ago, of trying to help three members of our family learn to drive. My daughter, who was the last to learn, wisely enlisted the help of a driving instructor. She was delighted with his attitude.

Whenever she did anything wrong, which was quite often at the beginning, he would include himself in her faults. 'When we came up to the last corner, we were going just that little bit *too* fast, weren't we?'

'For we do not have a high priest who is unable to sympathise with our weaknesses, but we have one who has been tempted in every way, just as we are – yet was without sin.' (Hebrews 4:15, NIV.)

The woman taken in adultery stood alone before Jesus after all the finger-pointing hypocrites had fled. 'Where are your accusers?' asked Jesus. 'They have gone, sir,' she replied. 'Then neither do I accuse you,' declared Jesus. 'But we're not going to do that again, are we?'

That's *my* version, of course. But d'you know? I'm not *really* sure!

Wrong cover

I remember a cartoon showing a salesman in a gents' out-fitters, standing behind a customer trying on a new jacket in front of a mirror. The salesman (behind the customer's back) is holding a fistful of bunched-up jacket and saying: 'It fits, Sir, perfectly!'

As a women's magazine art editor I took a lot of trouble choosing the front-cover picture. My pet theory was that there should be visual rapport between model and reader. The model, a pretty girl wearing a knitted garment, only needed to smile at the camera. But there are smiles and smiles. I wanted a homely smile, a nice-girl-next-door smile, and those are not easy to find.

One week we had a cover going through that I was pleased about. The smile was radiant. It would surely increase our readership. As it was going the rounds, collecting signatures of heads of departments before going to press, I noticed the fashion editor's initials next to a big question mark, drawing attention to a section of the photograph showing (to my absolute horror) a large safety pin bunching up a sizeable amount of garment.

The cardigan hadn't fitted the model!

We were 'Famed for its knitting'; but not any longer if that went through. I phoned the printers in great panic. Told them to stop work on the cover; a new one was following. I went hot and cold all over. An icy hand gripped the pit of my stomach. What kind of art editing was that? I'd made a ghastly mistake and felt so ashamed. Thankfully the editor didn't hear of it.

That night I slept fitfully and spent hours deliriously trying to take out safety pins from not just a few thousand copies, but the whole print run for one weekly issue. All 1.3 million!

I'd been obsessed, blinded by my 'smiling face', and committed that cardinal of sins in publishing – I'd assumed something was right without checking. Disaster had been averted, yet the potential, the enormity of a single mistake, appalled me.

Are you oppressed by the enormity of sin? Is the injunction: 'Sin no more' too hard? Christ's words should never be taken lightly. Knowing that we deliberately, habitually sin wounds the heart of our loving Saviour. To prolong that practice could have disastrous consequences (Hebrews 10:26, 27).

Don't lose heart or faith! Maybe we all have things in our lives that make entrance to God's kingdom the eye of a needle. Humanly speaking it is impossible – but not *with* God (Mark 10:27). God's grace is free, but never inadequate. Sufficient for all our needs. Made effective in weakness.

Life batters us, blows us off course; we'll even let go of God's hand. Yet 'Storms' (said George Herbert) 'make oaks take deeper root' – so hold on even tighter! God never willingly lets go. Nothing can separate us (Romans 8:38, 39).

Hungry?

'He has filled the hungry with good things, and the rich he has sent away empty.' (Luke 1:53, NKJV.)

When was the last time you were hungry? *Really* hungry, I mean. Not just a sharp appetite that can be stimulated by a long country walk before lunch, but the result of being systematically starved.

Several times I've had that 'Nil by mouth' sign hung over my hospital bed. Watched agonisingly as the rest of the ward tucked into meals, and after a 24-hour wait, frustratingly told that it was all in vain. Operation cancelled.

Statistically (so they say) at least 50% of the world's population suffers from malnutrition. The other half, presumably the so-called 'Western World', has too much food. Obesity is rife. A huge health problem. Many are also overweight and there's a thriving industry in slimming books.

If you're now a 'slim-celeb' who was formerly a 'fat-celeb' those shed pounds are worth their weight in gold! The media vie with one another and will bid vast amounts of cash for your story (and diet of course!).

Either way (over-nourished or under) it's not a joke. All need help.

The compulsive eater may have deep-seated emotional problems or possibly, as some scientists believe, it could be a physiological malfunction.

On the other hand anorexia nervosa is an obsessive psychological desire not to eat and put on weight.

What an amazingly mixed up world it is!

Half of our planet can't cope with more than enough food, and, apart from a few who are concerned, we seem content to let the other half die without it!

I don't know how this Lionel Blue joke fits into all this, but here it is:

A tramp said to a lady, 'I haven't eaten for a week.'

'Force yourself,' was her reply.

'Blessed are those who hunger and thirst for righteousness, for they will be filled.' (Matthew 5:6, NIV.)

What does it mean to 'hunger and thirst' for righteousness? J. B. Phillips says that it means one is happy, satisfied, to be filled with true goodness.

What is righteousness anyhow? Wise to what is right?

Apparently, 'righteousness' in Old Testament history was the twinning of two Hebrew words, sometimes rendered as 'justice'. Which also later came to mean conforming to the character of God himself.

In time emphasis was more on benevolent acts of generosity to the needy.

Righteous = bounteous.

' *"Be careful not to do your 'acts of right-eousness' before men, to be seen by them. If you do, you will have no reward from your Father in heaven."* ' (Matthew 6:1, NIV.)

Jesus is obviously using the word here not solely in the ethical, moral sense, but to stress its meaning as active, friendly deeds of goodness.

In modern parlance *proactive tlc!*

Mary in her *Magnificat*, her inspired song of praise to our Father God, said, ' *"He has filled the hungry with good things."* ' (Luke 1:53, NIV.)

Have *we*? As heirs to his Kingdom?

Why wait? If your heart tells you to *do it*.

But don't tell anyone (except of course your bank manager).

Conditions? Stipulations?
SMALL PRINT?

I'm really indebted to whoever wrote, 'Good works are not a condition for, but a consequence of salvation.'

With that in mind (or preferably in our hearts) why can't we say that God's love doesn't demand conditions, stipulations or requirements?

God's love yearns for consequences.

It's easy, however, to fall prey to scepticism. An ardent conditionalist has a very good weapon up his or her sleeve.

It's called *Repentance*.

'Surely,' it is said, 'repentance is a prerequisite for salvation.'

Look at Acts 2:38 and it does seem plausible. For after Peter's Pentecostal oration the people asked, 'What shall we do?' and Peter's reply was:

'Repent and be baptised, every one of you, in the name of Jesus Christ so that your sins may be forgiven.'

Call me obtuse if you like, yet I can't see repentance as a precondition for salvation. I see it as cause and effect. The spontaneous effect of an act.

God's act of love

His self-sacrifice on Calvary's Cross to save humanity from themselves. Surely Paul makes this same point, too, when he says that ' *"God's kindness leads you to repentance."* ' (Romans 2:4, NIV.)

Now free will may well be defined as acting without certain restraints. On the other hand, it can definitely only be actuated by motivation.

What motivation does God suggest to us?

' *"If you love me, keep my commandments."* ' (John 14:15, NKJV.)

Yes, there is a conditional clause here – it's IF. If we *love* God, that love will have an impact on our whole life. It will have an effect. There'll be an effectual change in our attitudes. The Decalogue which appeared to be full of stony prohibitions has now had its animosity melted down, softened by love.

We feel differently; changed. Yet there is no change in the Law. Christ has fulfilled its every requirement. The Law is not amended to allow for our weaknesses, our shortcomings, Our Advocate honours, upholds the Law.

Christ the Law-Giver, the Law-Creator, has always known that his Law has no legislation against those who believe. Those who have faith in his redemptive act of love and mercy. And it's only that love which can radically shift our viewpoint. A new viewpoint that will only take on its correct perspective as we kneel down humbly, submissively, in faith, allowing our Lord and Saviour to place himself between us and those ominous tablets of stone. Or if you prefer – that proverbial small print!

Keeping his commandments reverts from being a way to life to become a Way *of* Life – *his* Way of Life. A prescription for happiness – ours and our neighbour's happiness. Rules that are neither grievous (1 John 5:3) nor burdensome to keep because that is the way we respond and show the effect of his love. Christ's love is the *'very spring of our actions'* (2 Corinthians 5:14, JBP), and obedience is one of the many consequences of our love for him and his love for us (1 John 2:5).

Become an orchestrated fruit tree!
No experience necessary

*' "I am the vine; you are the branches. If a man remains in me and I in him, he will bear much fruit; apart from me you can do nothing."' * (John 15:5, NIV.)

What has conducting a symphony orchestra got to do with producing fruit?

Not a lot, admittedly, on the face of it. Say that *both*, metaphorically, create harmonious 'fruits', then we're on the way to valuing their compatibility.

Many years ago (when cruelly oblivious of the suffering I could inflict) I took up violin lessons. My teacher, who conducted a youth orchestra, invited me to join. I never got further than second fiddle. Content to play the 'um-pom-pom' bits instead of the 'tiddely-iddely' passages.

One Sunday afternoon a few of us were able to afford the cheaper seats at a town hall symphony concert, conducted by the famous Sir Adrian Boult. Not the best seats by any means; they were right at the back of the orchestra. Fine for us, because during the interval we could talk to some of the musicians. It felt just as if we were *in* the orchestra.

The timpanist, the chap on the drums, was friendly. He asked if we had any pennies. Pennies, then, were much bigger than now, and we fished some out of our pockets. He needed two, and he chose one that I had.

I can't remember exactly, but I think it was Elgar's *Enigma Variations* that was to be played after the break, and apparently there were instructions in the score asking for 'coins of the realm' to be put on the kettle drum. They gave precisely the sound Elgar wanted.

'What happens if you don't have any pennies?' we asked.
'Sir Adrian will give me a little frown,' he replied. 'He can

hear when they're not there, even if I can't. You watch his face.'

We did, and the gamut of all the expressions of emotion emanated not only from that conductor's face – but from his hands and body too. A tender, loving caress, sadness, jocularity, serenity and peace, passion.

That large group of musicians (usually ninety or more) had one focus of attention, were as one instrument, directed by one remarkable man!

In an orchestra, you have to keep one eye on the music and one eye on the conductor. The mood, the tempo changes unexpectedly. Sometimes there are hundreds of bars rest, silence for your particular instrument, but you still have to watch for your cue (it's so easy to lose your place).

Therefore the conductor's prompting glance is vital.

There are listeners in an orchestra, but they're not passengers, they're participants. The part they play may be insignificant, yet the maestro still values it. Their talents may bring them into the limelight – they may even become soloists – but they remain under the conductor's baton.

Some musicians admit that an outstanding conductor can draw out of them a quality of music that they never knew they were capable of playing. There's rapport. An invisible link between themselves and the conductor.

After that concert was over, my penny was returned with thanks. I kept it, cherished it for a long time, for it reminded me that even a penny, that coin of such a small denomination, could still play a part in a great work.

God's purpose is that we should play a part in his great work. We know what his work is, having seen it in the life of his only Son when he was on Earth. The Father's work – a ministry of healing and reconciliation. As Jesus said in John 14:10: ' *"It is the Father, living in me, who is doing his work."* '

Every true Christian knows, in his or her heart, the work that ought to be done. Just as the musician waits and watches for that vital, prompting glance, so does the follower of Christ listen for the prompting of the Holy Spirit, saying, 'Come in now and play your part!'

A Christian, by definition, is a living fruit true and not a prefabricated Christmas tree! But sadly, as we find in the parable of the fig tree (Luke 13:6-8) there is no future for a tree that does not bear fruit.

If a seed dies, it produces a good harvest (John 12:24). So Christ died, in order that we may live. *We* die, in order that Christ may live in us; draw out of us a quality we never dreamt we could possess. Share with us his divinity, in order that we may bear fruit for God! (Romans 7:4.)

Fruit, naturally, that is good, palatable and sweet. Not sour, sharp to the taste! God looked for good grapes in his vineyard (Isaiah 5:2) but found only wild, bad grapes! Galatians 5:22, 23 shows us the kind of fruit it should have been. *'But the fruit of the Spirit is love, joy, peace, patience, kindness, goodness, faithfulness, gentleness and self-control. Against such there is no law.'*

This fruit is in harmony with God's law because it's *from* God. Let *him* 'conduct' our lives. Let our heavenly Maestro draw out of us (for all stem from him, of course) that glorious 'harmonious fruit'. A feast for all senses!

Keep calm –
let go!

I was quite excited. At long last we were going to be able to pay off the mortgage on our house. It may not seem a large sum of money now – around £4,000 – but it was a lot to us at the time.

Late one afternoon I went to the building society office and asked the manager to calculate the exact figure I needed to pay. He disappeared and returned with our file.

'It'll be around £6,500,' he said with a smile.

'Around what?' I gasped.

He repeated the sum and showed me the details. There was something like an 'extended' or a 'second' mortgage taken out for a firm whose name I forget.

'Come back tomorrow morning, Mr Spearing,' suggested the suave, over-efficient manager. 'I'm sure when we work it out it'll be far less.'

My head was reeling. It didn't make sense.

That evening I dug out all the relevant correspondence. Had our solicitors overlooked some hidden pitfall? If they had, I couldn't find it.

I prayed, repeated every calming verse of scripture that I could remember; but it didn't help. I hardly slept a wink that night.

Next morning, tetchy, morose and irritable, I went back to the building society manager, whom I was beginning to dislike intensely.

He was still smiling. 'We've got it down to £6,323,' he announced smugly.

'Can I look at our file again,' I said.

I examined the roll number on the 'second' mortgage document. It almost tallied with ours apart from one figure!

'Gross incompetence!' I shouted hoarsely. 'This extra

mortgage is nothing to do with me. It's the wrong file!'

I could see others in the office looking across with interest. My lack of sleep resulted in a lack of control. I threw the proverbial book at him. Berated him with all the potential outcomes of such inefficiency. Suicide, heart attacks – the lot. He took it very quietly, like a lamb.

He'd failed; yet so had I.

I'd failed completely. Failed to trust God. Failed to take him at his word. Doubted his ability to look after my affairs. Made myself sick with worry.

I *know* that worry is useless. Downright destructive in fact. Look at Matthew 6:27, and we find Jesus asking us:

' *"Who of you by worrying can add a single hour to his life?"* ' (NIV.)

On the contrary, worry will undoubtedly cut short our lives, not by hours but by years! It's one of the most vicious contributory factors to ill health.

The life of a Christian is based on faith. Faith in Jesus Christ our Saviour. We live by that faith.

Except when we worry.

Yes, that's the snag. We'll accept the certainty of God's promise of life eternal, but not his promise of helping us with the crises of *earthly* life.

What's the secret?

I once saw a video showing a computer operator who was so incensed with the frustration, the problems, that his computer gave him, that he picked it up and hurled it at the office wall.

Why not try that metaphorically? Let go of your worries. Fling them in God's direction. He welcomes them.

' *You can throw the whole weight of your anxieties upon him, for you are his personal concern.*'

(1 Peter 5:7, JBP.)

What obligation?

For God, once he realised that the crowning glory of his creation had a design error, decided *not* to resign, but acknowledge his obligation to mankind by providing a remedy. He therefore gave his one and only Son, that whosoever believed in him should not perish but have eternal life.

What's wrong with that?

But before you give yourself an answer (and it's not a catch question) *think* (preferably with your heart). Because your answer may reveal how well you know your Father in Heaven.

To begin with, I'm not treading boldly over a theological minefield by suggesting that man was created *im*perfectly. He wasn't. In Genesis chapter 1 verse 27, we see that *'God created man in his own image,'* and in verse 31 that *'God saw all that he had made, and it was very good.'*

Very good.

Surely the greatest understatement in the whole Bible. Consider what science tells us about the complexities of the human body.

Life is a veritable miracle of creation!

In John 1:1 we read that *'the Word was with God, and the Word was God'*. And in verse 14: *'The Word became flesh and for a while lived among us.'*

If that means that God became man in order to redeem mankind, what does it mean for us? Created in the image of God?

Whatever word we use to describe that image, Paul tells the Colossians a surer way of understanding it. In chapter 3 verse 10 he points out that once we have accepted Christ as our Saviour, the old self, the old man of sin, our previous nature is in the process of being constantly renewed by God into his own image. God brings us to a fuller knowledge of himself.

That suggests that the lost image of God is in us, was (for want of a better word) his nature. Not a physical likeness. Christians know that only God is perfect and all have sinned and fall short of the glory of God (Romans 3:23, NIV).

To assert that God's creation of man was flawed is in fact to question the very character of God. According to Psalm 8:5 man was made *'a little lower than the heavenly beings'* (NIV).

Now we know that sin made its entry into this world through the one man, Adam; and it was that sin which brought death to the whole human race. God's image in man had been obliterated, for we find in Genesis 5:3 that Adam's son, Seth, was a son in his own likeness. Simplistically, it meant the emergence of self in man. Man's life was now predominantly selfish.

John R. W. Stott says: 'What someone wrote of an Englishman is true of every man: "*a self-made man who worships his creator*'."

Is it possible to sum up the image of God in one word? Hardly. Yet the apostle John does it in three gracious words: God is love (1 John 4:16).

Let's face reality. Does the world today accept that as truth? By no means. The world will not believe that selfishness could cause all its problems. It blames God for the disastrous state that man's *in*humanity has caused.

Man asks God to step in and do something, forgetting that he already has. Our Creator God sacrificed himself to save mankind from eternal death.

God's crowning glory of creation designed in error? No! Designed to reflect the love of our Creator! Life was destined for love-motivation. Love is the only arousal of love.

We love him because he first loved us. Read again the start of this article. Do you agree it's a travesty of the truth?

Did God have to acknowledge any obligation to man? Emphatically not!

A daughter has a baby of her own. She comes one day to her mother, hugs her, and says: 'Thanks, Mum, for fulfilling those necessary obligations to me when *I* was a child. I never realised that so many existed.'

'Obligations?' asked Mum. 'I was never aware of any. I just loved you!'

A red herring?

One of the most oft-quoted Bible texts to encourage (or even intimidate) the health-conscious Christian is: *'Know ye not that ye are the temple of God, and that the spirit of God dwelleth in you?'* (1 Corinthians 3:16, KJV.)

But this text, if used only in a health context, can be a slippery slope to discouragement. The inevitable inference is that unless you have a healthy body, God will not want to live in you, especially if you read verse seventeen: *'If anyone defiles the temple of God, God will destroy him. For the temple of God is holy, which temple you are.'* (NKJV.)

The causes of many illnesses can be laid on our own doorsteps, yet what about those burdened with genetically inherited, incurable diseases? Does God consider their bodies as unfit habitations for his presence? Deny them the privilege of being his temple?

Governmental spin-doctors are accused of burying their bad news among greater bad news. Are Christians misled by the arch spin-doctor, who does likewise with good news?

It's obviously wise to avoid intake of anything (food, drink or otherwise) that impairs our ability to work for God. But surely our primary concern when reading 1 Corinthians 3:16 should be to make, through the power of our Almighty God's more than sufficient grace, a heartfelt, conscious affirmation of its spiritual promise.

I can find no context for physical health in that verse, or in its counterpart in 1 Corinthians 6:19, 20. So is it a proverbial red herring?

A devious distraction?

I'm sure God longs for the invitation to live in us, regardless of any misgivings we may have of our physical worthiness.

A more in-depth study of 1 Corinthians, chapters 3 and 6,

reveals that Paul warns not against bodily defilement as such, but the corruption of worldly philosophy and sexual immorality. Physical health has never been a level playing field. With advancing age I feel personally that it's never felt so true that *'We have this treasure in* [fragile?] *earthen vessels, that the excellence of the power may be of God and not of us.'* (2 Corinthians 4:7, NKJV.)

Holman Hunt's painting *The Light of the World* shows Jesus standing outside a door with no latch. The means to open it are on the inside. The key granting God access into our hearts can surely only be our own free will.

Christ knocks (Revelation 3:20), but he will never force an entry. We have to make the decision to let him in. It's a sole (or even a soul) responsibility.

For you. For me.

'Once a man is united to God, how could he not live for-ever? Once a man is separated from God, what can he do but wither and die?' C. S. Lewis.

*Mis*representation

A s a schoolboy I used to pretend that I had a wide circle of female friends. Among my favourites were Miss Di Agnose, Miss Bea Gotten and Miss Em Ploy. Groans all round, of course, as soon as the penny dropped.

But it wasn't until I got my first job in publishing that I added another unpleasant girl to my list (and I'm not a *mis*ogynist!). She's that most awkward of customers – *mis*representation.

I was only a young sprog learning how to do layout on a weekly magazine and my art editor warned me – photographs could be *mis*leading. (Oh no! – they proliferate too!) Apparently there had been a great deal of bother about a published picture showing couples on a dance floor. A gentleman had written in to complain that he was in that photograph dancing with a lady who was not his wife!

This, he asserted, gave the impression to a very wide public that he was a philanderer. It could be – wait for it – *mis*construed. No more! I promise.

I can't remember the outcome, whether the magazine was sued or not. It's too long ago.

I can remember when little white rectangles were placed over people's eyes on television. Now there's a fuzzy ball superimposed over the faces of those allowed protection, and it follows them wherever they go (only on telly of course!). We are informed that this concealment is for 'legal reasons'.

Somewhere or other I read that verse one of Isaiah's sixtieth chapter, ' *"Arise, shine, for your light has come, and the glory of the Lord rises upon you"* ' was the motivation for artists to depict a halo, that disc or circle of light that's shown surrounding the head of a sacred person.

Painters of the Renaissance loved them and they took many forms. A silver, delicate wire-like ellipse, a beautiful, highly-decorated gold plate – for all the world hovering miraculously like a miniature UFO around the head of this or that 'saintly' personage.

Scientists tend to debunk haloes as a figment of the imagination or a trick of light. Yet the Bible tells us that the face of Moses shone after being with God (Exodus 34:29) and one of the priestly blessings given to the Israelites was *'the Lord make his face shine upon you'* (Numbers 6:25).

There's nothing to match the Transfiguration, however, when the clothes of Jesus became *'dazzling white, whiter than anyone in the world could bleach them'* (Mark 9:3, NIV).

Jesus Christ says, ' *"I am the light of the world. Whoever follows me will . . . have the light of life." '* (John 8:12.) His followers are encouraged in Matthew 5:16 to be 'shining examples! A devoted Christian will surely acknowledge that if there is any loveliness in his character it is not of himself, it can only come from Christ – the loving power of God living and shining from within him.

It's fascinating to watch those helicopter-mounted, thermal-imaging cameras used on TV's 'Police Camera Action'.

My imagination may be running riot, but I love to think that perhaps (only perhaps, mind you) God might have his own '*halo*-imaging camera'. A heavenly way of picking up the nimbus, the radiance, the Glory of the Lord that has, hopefully, risen upon us.

Now we know that the 'fuzzy ball' prevalent on TV documentaries conceals the identity of possible lawbreakers (and that could embrace all of us, I suppose). Interestingly there is a curious parallel in the King James Version of Isaiah 44:22, *'I have blotted out, as a thick cloud, thy transgressions.'* Likewise, the Wedding Garment of Matthew 22:11 – which is the imputed righteousness of Christ – hides our identity as lawbreakers (yet freely acquitted in the eyes of God in Romans 5:18, JBP). We're no longer God's enemies, but God's friends. He knows us personally.

He wants to break down the old barriers of estrangement. 'Let's talk, he says (Isaiah 1:18). So I try to, and he does give me a lot of advice. Yet I'm inclined not to listen carefully enough, and it's taken me a long time before I've understood. I've concluded that God is telling me to get rid of the mis(ses) in my life – the *mis*givings, the *mis*conceptions. They're all – without exception – minuses.

'What you need,' says God, *'is a plus in your life, and that plus is me!'*

'But Lord,' I remonstrate, 'my conscience tells me that I'll always be a *mis*representation of what you intended me to be.'

'You're right,' he replies, 'but that's not the point of the Gospel at all. The Good News is that I AM your representative. For legal reasons I do represent you. Whoever believes in me is not condemned.' (See John 3:18.)

Then in a quiet, almost inaudible voice: 'If that doesn't change your life completely – nothing will.'

It *has* changed my life.

Whenever I think of God's self-sacrifice for me I feel a warm glow in my heart. As long as it's warm and glowing, I know it's alive. It could be giving some light. So perhaps (only perhaps, mind you!) I can definitely say: 'My light has come.'